American Indian Music and Musical Instruments

American Indian Music and Musical Instruments

With instructions
for making the instruments

GEORGE S. FICHTER

Drawings and diagrams by Marie and Nils Ostberg

David McKay Company, Inc. New York

The music in this book is based on the
Bulletins of the Bureau of American Ethnology.

Library of Congress Cataloging in Publication Data

Fichter, George S
American Indian music and musical instruments.

Bibliography: p. 111
Includes index.
SUMMARY   Describes every category of Indian music
from war chants to music for curing illnesses. Includes
instructions and diagrams for making Indian musical
instruments, as well as the music and words for a number of Indian songs.
1. Indians of North America—Music—Juvenile
literature. 2. Musical instruments—Construction—Juvenile literature,   [1. Indians
of North America—Music. 2. Musical instruments—Construction]
I. Ostberg, Marie. II. Ostberg, Nils. III. Title.
ML3930.A2F44   781.7'2'97   77-14906
ISBN 0-679-20443-1

10 9 8 7 6 5 4 3 2

Manufactured in the United States of America

For Nadine,
who endures
better than I

CONTENTS

Map   viii

Major Indian Tribes of
    the North American Continent   ix

1. Those Who Were Here First   1
2. The Nature of Indian Music   9
3. Songs of Joy and Sorrow   19
4. War Songs   27
5. Curing Sickness with Songs   33
6. Songs for Good Hunting
    and Bountiful Crops   37
7. Lullabies   43
8. Love Songs   47
9. Death Songs   51
10. How to Make Indian
    Musical Instruments   55

Designs for Decorating Indian Musical
    Instruments   100

Table of Common Metric Equivalents
    and Conversions   110

Selected Bibliography   111

Index   113

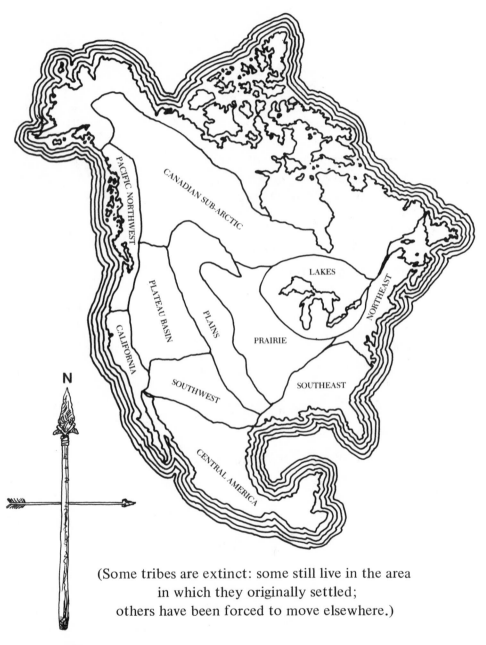

N

PACIFIC NORTHWEST

CANADIAN SUB-ARCTIC

LAKES

PLATEAU BASIN

PLAINS

NORTHEAST

CALIFORNIA

PRAIRIE

SOUTHWEST

SOUTHEAST

CENTRAL AMERICA

(Some tribes are extinct: some still live in the area
in which they originally settled;
others have been forced to move elsewhere.)

MAJOR INDIAN TRIBES OF THE NORTH AMERICAN CONTINENT

PACIFIC NORTHWEST

Bellabella
Bellacoola
Chinook
Haida
Klamath
Kwakiutl
Makah
Nootka
Quileute
Quinault
Salish
Tlinglit
Tsimshian

CALIFORNIA

Chumash
Costano
Hupa
Karok
Maidu
Mission
Miwok
Modoc
Pomo
Salinan
Shasta
Wintun
Yokuts
Yurok

SOUTHWEST

Acoma
Apache
Arizona Papago
Chiricahua Apache
Havasupai
Hopi
Maricopa
Navajo
Pima
Pueblo
Walapai
Yavapai
Yuma
Zuni

PLATEAU-BASIN

Bannock
Cayuse
Flathead
Gosiute
Kutenai
Mono
Nez Percé
Paiute
Panamint
Paviotso
Piegan
Shoshoni
Shuswap

Thompson
Ute
Washo
Yakima

PLAINS

Arapaho
Assinboin
Blackfoot
Cheyenne
Comanche
Crow
Gros Ventre
Kiowa
Sioux
Teton Sioux

PRAIRIE

Arikara
Dakota
Hidatsa
Illinois
Ioway
Kansas
Mandan
Miami
Missouri
Omaha
Osage
Oto
Pawnee
Ponca
Santee
Shawnee

Wichita
Yankton

LAKES

Chippewa
Fox
Kickapoo
Menomini
Ottawa
Pottawatomi
Sauk
Winnebago

SOUTHEAST

Alabamu
Apalachee
Atakapa
Biloxi
Caddo
Calusa
Catawba
Cherokee
Chickahominy
Chickasaw
Chitimacha
Choctaw
Creek
Koasati
Natchez
Powhatan
Quapaw
Seminole
Timucua
Tuscarora

NORTHEAST

Abnaki
Algonkian
Beothuk
Conestoga
Delaware
Erie
Iroquois
Leni-Lenape
Mohican
Malecite
Massachuset
Micmac
Nanticoke
Narragansett
Passamaquoddy
Pennacook
Penobscot
Pequot
Powhaton
Shinnecock

CANADIAN
SUB-ARCTIC

Algonkian
Beaver
Carrier
Chipewyan
Cree
Dogrib
Hare
Ingalik
Kaska

Khotana
Kutchin
Montagnais
Nahane
Naskapi
Sarsi
Satudene
Sekani
Slave
Tahaina
Yellow Knife

CENTRAL AMERICA

Aztec
Chorotega
Coahuntec
Concho
Huatec
Lacandones
Lagunero
Lenca
Maya
Mixtec
Mosquita
Olmec
Otomi
Papago
Quiché
Seri
Tarahumara
Tarascan
Toltec
Yaqui
Zapotec

1

Those Who Were Here First

Long before the arrival of Columbus, music rang out across America—from the deep forests of the East, over the vast prairies, to the rugged mountains of the West. People danced to the beat of drums or followed their rhythmic cadence while chanting ballads about their personal deeds and those of their ancestors. Women crooned lullabies to babies. Young people courted to the lilt of birdlike flutes. Old people sang songs to ready themselves for death. Like people who make music everywhere in the world, these American natives expressed triumphs and defeats, joys and sorrows through their sounds—and they gave thanks for blessings.

Who were these early Americans?

Columbus called them Indians. He believed his voyage

across the Atlantic to the west had brought him to the East Indies, so he named the people for the land on which he thought he had landed. But Columbus was half a world wrong. The islands he discovered were in the West Indies. He was sailing the waters of the New World—the Americas.

Despite this mistake in geography, Columbus was really not far wrong in calling the people Indians. They at least shared a common ancestry with the people of the land where Columbus thought he had landed. They had met Columbus halfway around the world, having made their share of the journey centuries earlier.

No one really knows precisely when or how these people came to America or where they made their crossing. A long-held belief is that they crossed at the Bering Strait between what are now Siberia and Alaska. But many present-day anthropologists and archaeologists believe they migrated northward from South America.

There is no way of knowing how many waves of Indians made migrations. But by the time Columbus arrived in 1492, an estimated thirteen million Indians inhabited the New World. About nine million lived in South America, three million in Central America and Mexico. In North America, there were a million.

Since the civilizations in Central and South America were much more advanced, it seems most likely that the Indians first settled in what is now Peru, in other parts of South America, and in Central America, and then migrated northward. Findings in recent years have indeed supported this theory, and it has also been demonstrated that it would have been possible to cross the Pacific in primitive boats or on rafts. Certainly there were across-the-Pacific contacts, which would explain some of the similarities in tools, crafts, and customs shared with people of the South Pacific. More is learned about this each year, but we may never know for certain how the migrations really came about.

By the time Columbus arrived, the Indians of North America had greater differences in languages and customs than occurred among all the peoples of Europe. They were divided into more than 300 tribes and spoke more than 150 languages. When members of unrelated tribes met, they could not understand each other, although most could communicate by the widely employed sign language.

The many tribes of Indians differed, also, in their ways of living. Some never progressed far beyond the customs of the Stone Age people. Some lived mainly by hunting and fishing or by harvesting wild fruits, berries, and roots. When hunting and foraging became poor, they moved. Other tribes were skilled farmers. They lived for many years in one place and built villages near their fields. Some tribes developed into civilizations that rivaled many existing in Europe during the same period in history. These centers of culture were most highly developed in Mexico and other parts of Central America and in South America, but some cultures spread as far north as the Mississippi Valley and eastward into what is now Georgia.

The Indian tribes of North America also held a variety of beliefs and customs. Though their ways of worship differed, one similarity prevailed: a reverence for nature. The air, land, and water; the game of the forest, the crops of the field, the fish from the streams, lakes, and sea—all were considered as gifts from the Great Spirit—the white man's term for the Indians' supreme power. Some Indians spoke directly to the Great Spirit. Others communicated through the plants, animals, stars, earth—all the works of the Great Spirit. The Indians gave thanks for all the goodnesses of the earth. Always they tried to live in harmony with the natural world of which they were a part, for to the Indians, nature was perfect. And they considered themselves only small elements of this perfection.

Early settlers called the American Indians "redskins," although none of the Indians really had red skin colors. Some were almost coppery brown, others yellowish, and still others coffee-colored. Some were tall and slim, others short and stocky. Some had narrow heads, sharp hawklike noses, high cheekbones, and thin lips. Others had broad faces, flat noses, and thicker lips. Most of them had straight black hair, but a few had wavy, brownish hair. It was these people of such varied features—most certainly the first Americans—that Columbus called Indians. But there never was a truly "typical" North American Indian.

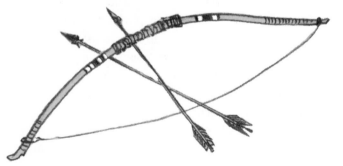

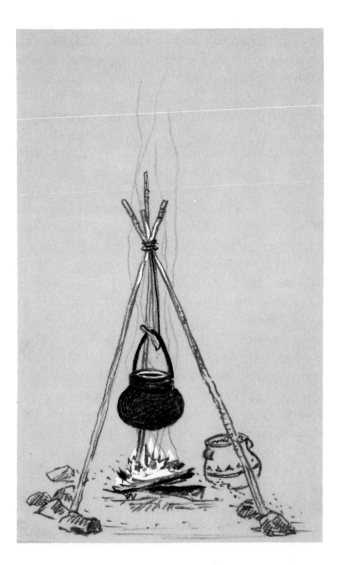

When the white man came to America, the Indians at first shared their world with him. They taught the white settlers how to bury a fish with their grains of corn to help the plants grow tall and to bear well. They showed the newcomers how to tap the maple trees to get the sugary sap and they gave

5

freely of their wisdom in the ways of the wilderness. The Indians were generous—sharing was one of their customs. But the Europeans had a different purpose in the New World. They wanted to claim the land and its riches for their countries.

Neither the Indians nor the white men ever took time to understand each other and the result was disastrous for the Indians. The Europeans quickly took advantage of the lack of organization among the different tribes. Soon the French had made alliances with some of the tribes and encouraged them to fight the Indians who had become friendly with the English or with the Dutch. The English and the Dutch countered. Meanwhile, more and more white men poured onto the North American continent and took the Indians' land by force. Some tribes were completely annihilated in battles against the Europeans. Others were killed by diseases brought to them by the white man.

For many years, the Indians were pictured primarily as cruel, savage, and warlike, seldom as a happy people who made music and sang songs. But all of the Indians had songs. Some were sung on special occasions or during ceremonies. Others were highly personalized; each person learned his or her personal songs and also those of the tribes. In this manner, the songs were passed from generation to generation. Many of these songs were lost when a tribe disappeared.

Fortunately, about a century ago, a few people were wise enough to begin collecting some Indian songs. With the invention of the phonograph, they also made records. What we do know about authentic Indian music today is largely the result of their pioneering work.

Among the several people who collected and recorded the songs of various Indian tribes in the late 1800's and early 1900's were Natalie Curtis and Frances Densmore. Their outstanding work is the source of many of the songs in this

book. But as every student of Indian music points out, much of the poetry of the original song is lost when the Indian words are translated into English. Often, for example, it requires many English words to give the meaning of a single Indian word. The rhythmic beauty of the original cannot be preserved. But in the following chapters, we will be concerned mainly with why the Indians sang and with the kinds of instruments they played.

At the end of the book, you will find a section on how to make replicas of several kinds of Indian musical instruments and a table of common metric conversions and equivalents.

The Nature of Indian Music

Indians from unrelated tribes spoke different languages, but in most cases, they understood each other's songs. Even though words might be meaningless, the rhythms of the different types of songs were much the same from tribe to tribe. Music formed a bond that transcended the centuries to their common ancestry.

To the Europeans, the rhythms and melodies of Indian music were unfamiliar and pagan, not easily appreciated when compared to their own kind of music. Some of the Indian music does indeed have a mysterious, almost hypnotic quality that can cast a sort of spell over the listener.

All of the songs of the Indians had a purpose. They did not sing or play their instruments for audiences. Rather, they

sang to their spirits—asking for help or giving thanks. To the Indians, singing and music were not considered as performances but as a part of life itself. There was a song for every ceremony or special occasion and also for marking all of the important steps in an individual's life. It was not unusual for an Indian to know several hundred songs and to be able to repeat each of them perfectly.

Some of the songs were made by man: that is, they were deliberately created in his mind or his thoughts. They were sung to please the ear while at the same time expressing feelings. They stirred Indians to perform great deeds in hunting or in war, giving them the strength to meet danger, to endure pain, and to face even death bravely. But most songs originated in dreams or visions. Because the Indians believed they came from a supernatural source, they had great powers and were considered holy. Such a song became the Indian's personal property. The person owned not only the song but also its powers and no one else could sing it without the owner's permission. Sometimes the Indian would sell the right to sing the song to someone who especially liked the words and the power it commanded.

When the Indians sang together in ceremonials, each person had to be able to sing all of the words without making an error. If a mistake was made, the singing was stopped and the song was started again at the beginning. A mistake was an insult to the Great Spirit or to the supernatural power whose services were being called upon, but who might also steer his great powers in the wrong direction. Carelessness could not be tolerated with songs that were holy.

In singing, Indians held their lips tight and produced the sounds in their throats. Often they ended notes in long quavers. In tone, their voices ranged from falsetto to bass. The style of singing differed from one region to another and tended to imitate subtly the sounds of nature: the hoot of an owl or the howl of a wolf or a coyote. When the Indians sang in a group, all carried the same melody, but because of differences in voice tones, there was sometimes a harmonic effect. Women commonly joined in the ceremonial songs, keeping their voices an octave higher than the men's.

Not all of the Indians were good singers. Some had hoarse voices, as rasping as a crow's call or the croaking of a frog. Others seemed to howl like coyotes. A few were excellent singers, their notes as true and as melodious as a bird's. But the quality of the voice really did not matter greatly. Most important was the meaning of the song and the accuracy with which it was sung.

The Indians of the Pacific Northwest sometimes participated in song contests. The different tribes, or clans, competed to see which could remember the most songs and also who could sing, without a mistake, a song he or she had just heard for the first time. But most tribes did not generally sing their songs at such pleasure gatherings.

Indian instrumental music was an accompaniment or background for singing but it did not often match the rhythm of the song itself. Thus an Indian would sing in one rhythm while the drum was thumped in another. Sometimes Indians danced to still a third rhythm and when they danced, they used all of the muscles in their bodies, not just their legs. All of this was much different from the European concept of what constitutes good music. It was also a considerable feat. Try it sometime. It is much like patting your head while simultaneously rubbing your stomach and drumming with your fingers.

The Indians made their musical instruments with materials that were available to them. The most widely used instrument was the drum, which was made in many shapes and sizes. Some drums were made for use only in particular

ceremonies and were played only when that ceremony was repeated. Some drums were very large and loud; others were small and muted. The head of a drum was usually made of a buffalo or deer hide scraped thin and stretched tight across the top or opening. The hollowness of the drum served to amplify the sound when the drum was struck.

Tom-toms were small drums that were held in the hand. Most tom-toms had heads on only one end. A few smaller drums had heads on both ends. Big war drums, or *tombes,* were usually made of hollowed sections of large trees that measured several feet in diameter. Some of these drums were made of hollowed logs five or ten feet long, and they were big enough to be played by several Indians at the same time. Other drums had such strong heads that the Indians could dance on top of them and pound out rhythms with their feet. These big drums were often placed over pits in the ground to help amplify their sounds. Sometimes they were supported on three or four stakes.

13

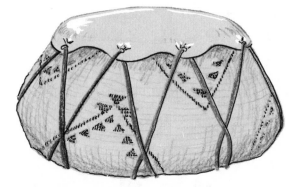

Indians of the Southwest stretched hides over the tops of pots, baskets, and bowls to make their drums. To get different tones, they put water in the containers; they could change the sound of a drum by varying the level of the water. Other Indians used the hollow shells of turtles as drum resonators. Indians of the Pacific Northwest made an all-wood square, or box, drum on which they sat and kicked or pounded it while they sang. Still other tribes beat on wooden planks to make a resounding, drumlike noise. Almost without exception, all of the various kinds of drums were highly decorated, as were the drumsticks, or thumpers.

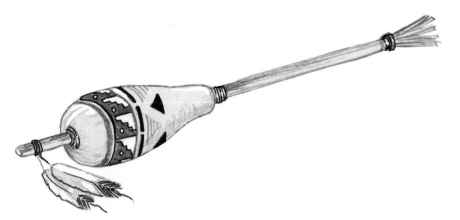

Rattles were also popular. Some consisted only of bags of buckskin in which pebbles, seeds, or sand were put to make a rattling noise. Others were made of hollow wood, horn, or shells. The most common rattles were dried gourds filled with pebbles or other objects. Many had handles and were held while the Indian sang or danced. Others were strapped to the legs just below the knee and were shaken as the Indian danced. Some tribes fastened rattles to the sides of their drums to make more noise when they beat the instruments.

Rhythmic noises were also part of Indian music. The Indian carved notches in a stick, then drew another stick, or

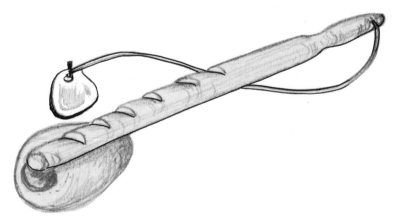

the flat shoulderblade bone of a deer or some other animal across the notches. In the Southwest, the notched stick was placed on a hollow gourd to amplify the noise. Sometimes shells or colored rocks were hung from sticks and then allowed to strike each other to make a noise. Indians of the Pacific Northwest made a clapper by splitting a stick and then striking it against their palm.

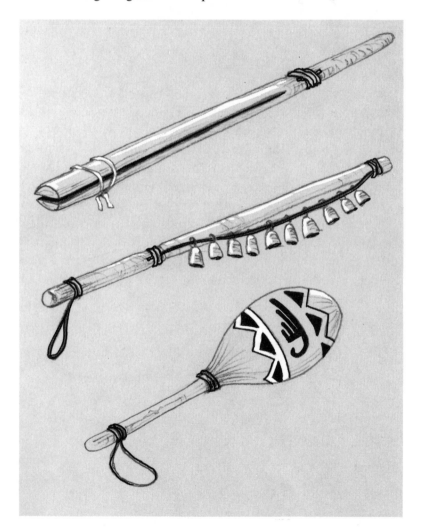

Flutes and whistles were fashioned by many tribes. The whistles were usually carved from the wingbone of a bird, preferably an eagle. An Indian whistle had no stops, so it produced only one tone that could be varied only slightly by changing the force or the direction of the air blown into it. Most whistles were used primarily as signaling devices, not as musical instruments. Flutes were hollow reeds or wood in which the center was reamed or burned out. The Dakota Sioux were excellent flutists whose instruments were mostly of cedar. Most flutes had two or more holes so that different notes could be played. Since the Indians did not regulate the placement of these holes, each instrument was slightly different. Some Indians of the Southwest made panpipes, much like those used in China. They consisted of two, three, or four flutes of different lengths and tones, joined together horizontally.

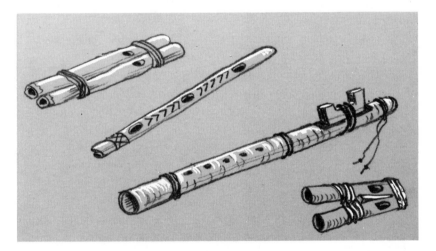

Only the Apache of the Southwest and the Maidu of California had stringed instruments, which they adopted from Mexican tribes. They played a kind of primitive fiddle with one or more strings across which a bow was drawn. The strings were usually made of horsehair, but some were made

17

of thin, tightly stretched rawhide. The largest of these fiddles was about five feet long and had a head that was a foot or more wide, usually fashioned from the trunk of an agave plant. These big fiddles produced a deep, sonorous tone, much like the bellowing of a bull alligator.

Songs of Joy and Sorrow

Books, television, and movies often portrayed the Indians as expressionless and virtually without emotion, except when they vented their anger and hostility on the warpath. This has become the Indians' stereotype. But in truth, although they were indeed quite stoic, the Indians were filled with joys and sorrows, just as any other peoples. They displayed these deeper feelings most clearly in their songs and music.

Weddings were gala events in many Indian tribes. Everyone in the village was invited to the ceremony and the feasting that followed it. This is demonstrated in the verses of a wedding song of the Malecite tribes, who lived in the Northeast.

Hey, ho, dance away,
   Dance away!
Hey, ho, dance away,
   Dance away!
   Dance away!
Harder, faster let us go.
   Dance away!
   Dance away!
Youths and maidens, be gay,
   Dance away!
Youths and maidens, be gay,
   Dance away!
Faster and faster, let us go.
   Dance away!
Come, come, come, come!

Indian women sang to make their work lighter and to give thanks for their food. Women of the Zuni chanted the following joyful song as they ground corn:

O, my lovely mountain,
   To'yallanne!
O, my lovely mountain,
   To'yallanne!
   To'yallanne!
High up in the sky,
See Rain-Makers seated,
Hither come the rain-clouds now,
   He-ya, ha-ya, he-ya!
Behold, yonder
All will soon be abloom
Where the flowers spring—
Tall shall grow the youthful corn plants.

When young Zuni girls were given the job of grinding corn, the young boys sometimes entertained them with songs. This one tells them to be happy because the rains will bring more work.

Lovely! See the cloud, the cloud appear!
Lovely! See the rain, the rain draw near!
  Who spoke?
'Twas the little corn ear
High on the tip of the stalk
Saying while it looked at me
  Talking aloft there—
"Ah, perchance the floods
  Hither moving—
Ah, may the floods come this way!"

All of the songs were not happy, of course, for the Indians also had times of sorrow. In this sad song of the Dakota Sioux, a mother is called to return from the dead because her small son still cries for her.

> *Mother, oh come back,*
> *Mother, oh come back,*
> *Little brother calls as he seeks*
> *   thee, weeping.*
> *Little brother calls as he seeks*
> *   thee, weeping.*
> *Mother, oh come back,*
> *Mother, oh come back!*
> *Saith the Father,*
> *Saith the Father.*

Nor were all of the songs for the young. Old Cheyenne warriors sometimes climbed to the top of a hill at dawn and chanted this song over and over again.

> *He, our Father,*
> *He hath shown His mercy unto me.*
> *In peace I walk the straight road.*

Yuma Indians sang a happy song about the mockingbird.

Thin little clouds are spread
Across the blue of the sky,
Thin little clouds are spread—
Oh, happy am I as I sing.
I sing of the clouds in the sky.

Thus tells the bird.
'Tis the mockingbird who sings,
And I stop to hear,
For he is glad at heart
And I will listen to his message.

Then up the hill,
Up the hill I go my straight road,
The road of good—
Up the hill I go my straight road,
The happy road and good.

The following Navajo song expresses the Indians' joy of living. The song, which had many verses, was sometimes sung to people who were ill to help them realize that they would one day be perfect and live in a perfect world.

All is beautiful,
All is beautiful,
All is beautiful, indeed.
Now the Mother Earth
And the Father Sky,
　　Meeting, joining one another,
　　Helpmates ever, they.
All is beautiful,
All is beautiful,
All is beautiful, indeed.

SIOUX SONG OF THANKSGIVING
TO THEIR TRIBAL GOD.

Wa-Kan-tan-Ka   hears us, when we pray to him.

Wa-Kan-tan-Ka   loves us, when we do good   deeds.

He is strong and   truth—ful, Bless—ings he will   give.

Wa-Kan-tan-Ka   grants us   ev'—ry thing that's good.

4

War Songs

To the white settlers, the sound of the Indians' drums meant trouble. Their steady, ominous beat told them that the Indians were on the warpath and an attack was soon to follow. True, the Indians did use their drums to signal each other and to rally warriors from afar to join them in battle. And the drums also beat out the rhythm of war songs.

But their war songs were basically prayers in which they asked the Great Spirit for courage in battle and for a victorious and safe return. To the beat of the drums, often in a gradually increased tempo hour after hour, the Indians chanted their war songs. As time passed, they often worked themselves into a fervor as they readied themselves to meet the enemy.

The following portion of a Pawnee war song is typical of the chants sung by young Indian warriors preparing themselves for battle. The song is actually a prayer to the Pawnee God, *Tirawa,* for guidance and protection.

> *O, Great Expanse of the blue sky,*
> *See me roaming here,*
> *Again on the warpath, lonely;*
> *I trust in you. Protect me!*

Some war songs paid tribute to warriors who had been successful in years gone by and thus challenged young warriors to match their deeds. This song, for example, was sung to stir Winnebago braves to do as well as an older warrior who had earned the high honor of being allowed to wear an eagle's feather in battle.

> *Follow him, mount your horses!*
> *Follow him, mount your horses!*
> *Follow him, mount your horses!*
> *Follow him, mount your horses!*
> *He killed many!*
> *He hunts eagle feathers now!*
> *Follow him, mount your horses!*

Cheyenne warriors sang of leaving their slain enemy on the ground to be feasted on by the wolves. These braves pictured themselves as being clever as the wolf in hunting.

> *Ho yo! Hear ye! Come ye! Feast ye!*
> *O wolves!*
> *Feast, be ye merry,*
> *Yo, ho, gather*
> *At the dawn.*

For most young Indian braves, setting out to war was an adventure, an opportunity to accomplish great deeds. Success at war was a mark of manhood. Always, however, they attributed their powers, skill, and success to the Great Spirit. When they headed off to war, the Indians of some tribes painted their faces red. When they returned victorious, their faces were sometimes painted black with ashes, for black to the Indians was generally a good omen. Those who stayed behind, afraid to go to war, wore red paint, too. Cheyenne braves, returning from battle, chided them with this song:

> *Who are these*
> *Who stand and gaze at us?*
> *Who are these*
> *With red paint thick upon them?*
>   *By day*
> *In the sight of all men*
> *Went we forth to war!*

A lonely and homesick Kiowa brave sang this song to his fellow-warriors to lift their spirits and remind them that someone waited for them while he had no one.

> *O, you warriors, you have loved ones*
> *Longing for you, longing for you.*
>   *Rich are ye.*
> *O, you lovers, you have maidens*
> *Longing for you; none have I.*
> *Wherefore droop ye in silence, so downcast?*
>   *Cheer your hearts with song, ho!*

Before Pawnee braves went off to war, they asked for help from the Great Spirit with this chant to which they danced as they repeated the words again and again:

> *O Father, thou dost rule supreme,*
> *O Father, thou dost rule supreme,*
> *O Father, thou dost rule supreme,*
> *None greater, thou dost rule supreme.*
> > *Can there be any over thee?*
> > *O Father, can there greater be than thou?*
> *None greater, thou dost rule supreme.*

While Indian women did not go to war, they often sang songs to encourage their warriors to be brave in battle and also to give them confidence and strength in their encounters with the enemy. The women also lamented the absence of their lovers, as in this song sung by Kiowa maidens:

> *I have but one love,*
> *I have but one love,*
> *I have but one love,*
> *And he is far away*
> *On the warpath, e-ye, e-ye!*
> *Lonely are the days and weary.*

When the warriors returned victorious, the women greeted them. Pawnee women sang the following song to the braves returning from battle:

> *They are coming,*
> *They are coming!*
> *Lo, the victor host, ya he—Yo!*
> *Forth to meet them go the women*
> *With the rising sun, ya he—Yo!*
>
> *Cries a maid,*
> *Had but the Father made me man,*
> *O then might I have been like these*
> *Who now are coming,*
> *With the rising sun, ya he—Yo!*

Warriors of the Dakota Sioux tribe readied themselves for battle with this song:

> *Comrades, kinsmen,*
> *Now have ye spoken thus,*
> *The earth is mine,*
> *'Tis my domain.*
> *'Tis said, and now anew I exert me!*

The Indians were unquestionably dedicated in battle. They fought to win without regard to what might happen to them personally. Their songs helped to prepare them for whatever the outcome; many conveyed the same message as these lines from a war song of the Sioux:

> *It is bad to live to be old.*
> *Better to die young*
> *Fighting bravely in battle.*

SONG FOR RETURNING PAWNEE WARRIORS

Curing Sickness with Songs

To the Indians, the word "medicine" had a different meaning from the one white people knew. Most Indians believed there was both good medicine and bad medicine. And "medicine" was a mysterious kind of "luck" that was controlled by supernatural forces.

The Indians of some tribes always carried their medicine—a collection of rocks, roots, bark, herbs, and other objects that had been revealed to them in a dream or a vision. They claimed that the medicine was good luck, assuring them of success and safety as long as the charms were with them. Most medicine charms were small and could be carried in a bag, usually hung around the neck or fastened to a belt. But if the dream or vision prescribed larger objects, even unwieldy ones, the Indian was obliged to tote them anyhow, and he carried them in a large sack on his back.

When an Indian's medicine no longer seemed to work and his luck turned bad over a long period, the hapless fellow often fasted for days, hoping for a new dream or vision to give him a change in medicine. And sometimes, too, he would try to get special medicine when he was going on a hunting trip or on the warpath.

Illness was the result of bad medicine. Sometimes the Indians would try to cure themselves with herbs or potions, but usually they called for help from a Shaman, or medicine man. Shamans were specialists in healing by the use of supernatural powers and through their considerable knowl-edge of herbs. A Shaman might give his cure in a private ritual, or he might make the treatment in a ceremony attended by many people that lasted for days. In each case, music and songs were important. Both the medicine men and their assistants beat drums and shook rattles while they chanted special songs that had come to them from a supernatural source. Often the songs called on all of the spirits to join together in bringing about a healing and to scatter the disease "like the leaves of the forest" until it disappeared. When an old warrior of one of the Great Plains tribes became critically ill, a Shaman usually put a tom-tom directly over the warrior's head and then beat loudly on the tom-tom to drive away the sickness. The process continued until the patient either recovered or died.

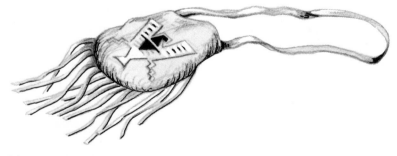

The Navajo sang for seriously ill tribal members in order to prepare them for a journey to a holy place where they would find everlasting peace. The following song actually had many verses. Each verse was sung four times, as the Indians first faced East and then West, North, and South.

Swift and far I journey,
Swift upon the rainbow.
Swift and far I journey,
Lo, yonder, the Holy Place!
    Yea, swift and far I journey.
To Sisnajinni, and beyond it,
    Yea, swift and far I journey
The Chief of Mountains, and beyond it,
    Yea, swift and far I journey;
To Life Unending, and beyond it,
    Yea, swift and far I journey;
To Joy Unchanging, and beyond it,
    Yea, swift and far I journey.

A medicine man of the Dakota Sioux sang the following in ceremonies of healing. The song was said to have come originally from a "holy man" who appeared once, then was never seen again.

O ye people, be ye healed;
Life anew I bring unto ye.
O ye people, be ye healed;
Life anew I bring unto ye
Through the Father over all
Do I thus.
Life anew I bring unto ye.

35

CHEYENNE SONG OF HEALING

By night I   go on my way   un—seen——

Then am I ho—ly, then have I pow—er   to heal.

Then am I ho—ly,   then have I pow—er to heal.

Hai yo he yo hai   yo—e yo e e   hai yo!

6

Songs for Good Hunting
and Bountiful Crops

The woodland Chippewa tribes' songs asked the spirits for a good flow of maple syrup. The Sioux and other tribes of the plains and prairies chanted for successful buffalo hunts. In the Southwest, the Hopi danced and sang for rain to help their crops grow. All Indians called upon the spirits for good hunting and bountiful crops with music and songs.

Some of the songs were simple, repetitive chants. Dakota hunters, for example, pledged in prayer that if they were spared from starvation by good buffalo hunting, they would first give their dogs a feast. They did find the buffalo, and so to fulfill their promise, they gave their dogs the choice pieces before eating any of the buffalo meat themselves. And while the dogs ate, the hunters chanted the following over and over:

May you feast well, O dog!

They intoned this same chant, or prayer, before they set out on a hunt, for they believed that if the dogs ate well, the tribe would have food aplenty, too.

The Navajo hunters sang several verses of the following before starting out on a hunt.

Comes the deer to my singing,
Comes the deer to my song,
Comes the deer to my singing.

He, the blackbird, he am I,
Bird beloved of the wild deer.
Comes the deer to my singing.

From the Mountain Black,
From the summit,
Down the trail, coming, coming now,
Comes the deer to my singing.

Through the blossoms,
Through the flowers, coming, coming now,
Comes the deer to my singing.

Through the pollen, flower pollen,
Coming, coming now.
Comes the deer to my singing.

Starting with his left forefoot,
Stamping, turns the frightened deer.
Comes the deer to my singing.

Quarry mine, blessed am I.
In the heat of the chase
Comes the deer to my singing.

To the Pueblo, Hopi, Zuni, and other tribes who lived in the desert lands of the Southwest, the greatest blessing was rain. In ceremonials that sometimes lasted for days, they sang and danced, as they asked for rain to fall on their parched fields.

Far as man can see
Comes the rain.
Comes the rain with me.

From the Rain-Mount,
Rain-Mount far away,
Comes the rain.
Comes the rain with me.

O'er the corn,
O'er the corn, tall corn,
Comes the rain.
Comes the rain with me.

Indians throughout North America grew corn, a mainstay in their diets, and nearly all the tribes had songs and rituals in which the spirits were called upon to assure them a good crop. The following is a typical corn-dance song:

Let the thunder be heard,
O ye Ancients!
Let the sky be covered with white blossom clouds,
That the earth, O ye Ancients,
Be covered with many colored flowers

That the seeds come up,
That the stalks grow strong,
That the people have corn,
That happily they eat.
Let the people have corn to complete the road of life.

40

In some ritual songs, the Shaman, or medicine man, did most of the singing. In the following song, he sang the first verse, then all tribe members sang the second. The Shaman sang the third verse, the others the fourth, and so on.

Behold! Our Mother Earth is lying here.
Behold! She giveth of her fruitfulness.
Truly, her power she giveth to us,
Give thanks to Mother Earth who lieth here!

We think of Mother Earth who lieth here.
We know she giveth of her fruitfulness.
Truly, her power she giveth to us,
Our thanks to Mother Earth who lieth here!

Behold on Mother Earth the spreading tree!
Behold the promise of her fruitfulness!
Truly her power she giveth to us,
Give thanks to Mother Earth who lieth here!

We see on Mother Earth the spreading tree.
We see the promise of her fruitfulness.
Truly, her power she giveth to us,
Our thanks to Mother Earth who lieth here!

PAPAGO CROP-SOWING SONG

There he   sits and   with his   pow—er,

He brings the South Wind toward   us.

Af—ter the   wind, he   brings the   clouds,

Af—ter the   clouds, he brings the   rain.

That makes all our crops grow, ————————

That makes all   our crops   boun—ti— ful.

7

Lullabies

While the men sang loudly and vigorously, often with a nasal quality, Indian women sang songs to lull their young to sleep or to soothe them when they were uncomfortable. Many of the Indian men were not impressed by the lullabies. One said, "Women make a noise to put children to sleep, but it is not singing." But the women paid no attention because their lullabies worked.

Hopi women sang this song when their children cried and fussed. The owls in the song were a threat, but the mother's soothing voice made the children feel secure.

Owls, owls,
Big owls and little,
Staring, glaring, eying each other.
Children, from your boards,
Oh, see!
Now the owls are looking at you,
Looking at you.
Saying, any crying child,
Yellow eyes will eat him up.
Sleep, do not cry,
Sleep, do not cry.
Oh children, look,
Then we will pass you by.
Me-e, hoo, hoo, hoo, hoo, hoo.
A-ha, i hii, a-ha, i hi hi.
Hoo, hoo, hoo, hoo, hoo.

Cheyenne women sang a simple lullaby, repeating it softly again and again until their children fell asleep.

Little good baby,
He-ye,
Sleepy little baby,
A-ha h'm.

When a Kiowa mother left her child with an older woman while she went hunting, the babysitter used these words to put the child to sleep.

Hush thee, child—
Mother bringeth an antelope,
And the tidbit shall be thine.

Arapaho mothers also sang a soothing lullaby to their babies.

Go to sleep,
Baby dear, slumber,
Baby sleep,
Sleep, sleep, baby sleep.
Sleep, baby, sleep
Baby dear, slumber,
Baby sleep.

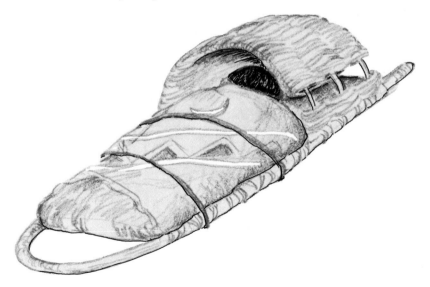

PASSAMAQUODDY LULLABY

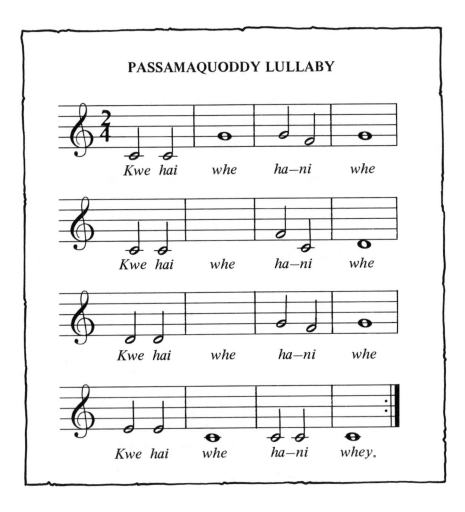

8

Love Songs

An older Indian once said, "If a brave begins to sing love songs too much, we send for a medicine man." He was making fun of young warriors who were courting, forgetting that once he sang such songs himself. Some Indian braves used the flute to lure the maiden of their choice, while others wooed their loves with songs that expressed their feelings.

In the long, cold winters of the Northeast, a Malecite brave setting out on a hunting trip that would last until spring, sang this song to the maiden he hoped would wait for him.

> *Look oft up the river, look oft and oft.*
> *In spring at the breaking of the ice, look oft;*
> *You may see me coming down in my canoe.*
> *Look oft up the river. Look anew, anew.*

A Dakota Sioux maiden confessed her love with this song:

> *Many are the youths, many youths.*
> *Thou alone art he who pleaseth me.*
> *Over all I love thee.*
> *Long shall be the years of parting!*

The wind song of the Kiowa women was a similar declaration of love.

> *I have but one love,*
> *I have but one love,*
> *I have but one love,*
> *And he is far away*
> *On the warpath, e-ye, e-ye!*
> *Lovely are the days and weary.*

When a Winnebago maiden awoke from a dream about an Indian temptress who had exceptional love powers, she believed that the powers had been passed to her in the dream and she sang this song:

> *Whomsoever look I upon,*
> *   He becomes love-crazed;*
> *Whomsoever speak I unto,*
> *   He becomes love-crazed.*
> *Whomsoever whisper I to,*
> *   He becomes love-crazed.*
> *All men who love women,*
> *Them I rule, them I rule,*
> *   My friend.*
> *Whom I touch, whom I touch,*
> *   He becomes love-crazed.*

MANDAN LOVE SONG OF THE FLUTE

Death Songs

The "happy hunting ground" was the white man's description of the Indians' heaven, or hereafter. Almost every tribe had a slightly different notion of the place where they would find eternal peace and happiness, where they hoped to continue to live the same sort of life as on earth, but in complete harmony. In many tribes, the dead were cremated and all of their personal belongings were burned at the same time.

For most Indians, death represented only a journey into a different life and was not feared. When Indians became old, they prepared themselves for death, often with personal songs. The well-known nature writer and painter, Ernest Thompson Seton, recorded one such song of an Indian Chief:

I, Chaska, do sing:
I care not where my body lies,
My soul goes marching on.
I care not where my body lies,
My soul goes marching on.

Death did not always wait for the old. When an Apache Chief and four of his warriors were cornered in a cave by a regiment of white soldiers for more than four days, they suffered from hunger and thirst. But they did not surrender. Instead, they prepared for their death and then rode out

bravely to face the rain of bullets from a hundred rifles.
Their story became legendary. Their death song was:

> *Father, we are going out to die.*
> *For ourselves we grieve not,*
> *But for those who are left behind.*
> *Let not fear enter into our hearts.*
> *We are going out to die.*

WINNEBAGO DEATH CHANT

Whom, oh Whom, Shall I now call Grand moth—er?

Whom, oh Whom, Shall I now call Grand moth—er?

Pe—za— Ga no—ni— ka ya— ge—che— ne—ze!

Pe—za— Ga no—ni— ka ya— ge—che— ne—ze!

10

How to Make Indian Musical Instruments

You can construct simple Indian musical instruments with readily available materials. Some that you can make will be exactly like those made by the Indians many centuries ago. Others can be fashioned with modern-day materials, but will nevertheless look and sound like those originated by the Indians. As a matter of fact, if the Indians were making these instruments today—and some do—they would not manufacture them precisely as their ancestors did. After all, deer hides, horn, eagle feathers, and similar items are now illegal or hard to come by.

Latter-day Indians were quick to change their customs to take advantage of materials they found around them. They shaped flutes out of gun barrels or pieces of pipe rather than bone or wood; they converted empty lard cans and wooden kegs into drums.

CARVING GUIDE

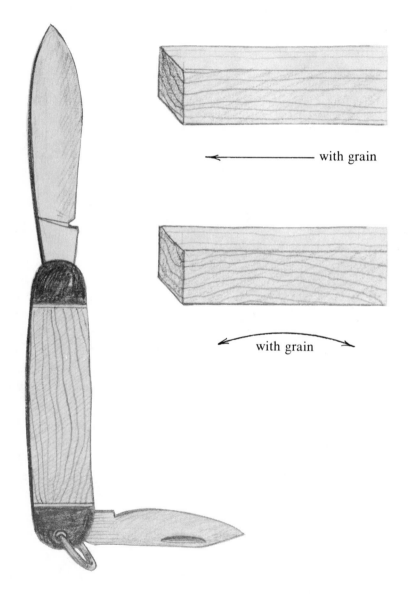

with grain

with grain

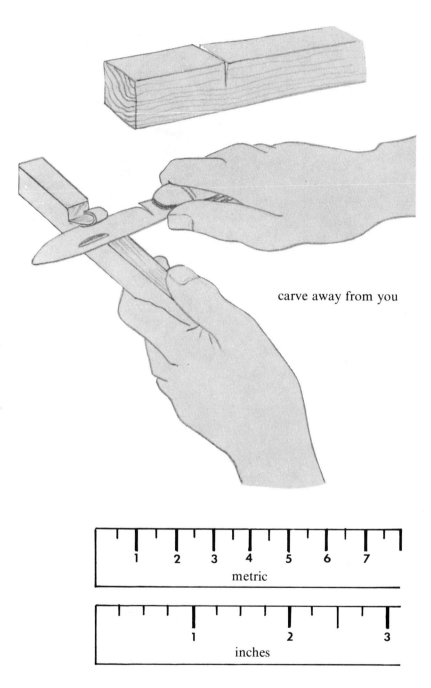

carve away from you

metric

1 2 3 4 5 6 7

inches

1 2 3

ORNAMENTAL GOURD RATTLES

A rattle, like a drum, simply makes a noise. Basically, it consists of some sort of container in which objects are placed that hit against each other and also against the sides of the container. Indians made their rattles from a variety of materials—gourds, horns, rawhide, shells, and tree bark. Gourd rattles, very popular among the tribes of the Southwest, were painted with designs in earth colors, black, and white; the thong wrist straps were decorated with feathers.

Materials

2 ornamental gourds, each approximately the
    same size
2 straight branches or 2 wooden dowels, each
    approximately 10″ long
small pebbles
twine, 36″ long
several small feathers
sharp penknife
ruler
pencil
paints (tempera or acrylic)
paint brush
white glue
wire coat hanger
sandpaper
fixative (optional)
handsaw (optional)

1. Cut or saw off the necks of each gourd, leaving a hole approximately 3/4″ in diameter in each gourd. Make another hole of the same size in the opposite end of each gourd, as shown in Fig. 1.

Figure 1

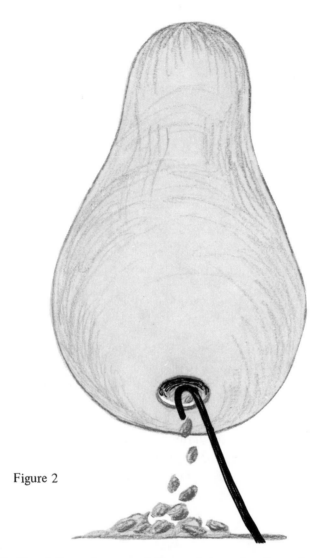

Figure 2

2. Bend the wire coat hanger into a hook and use it to scrape out the seeds in each gourd, as shown in Fig. 2.

3. When the insides of the gourds are thoroughly dry, place the pebbles in them.

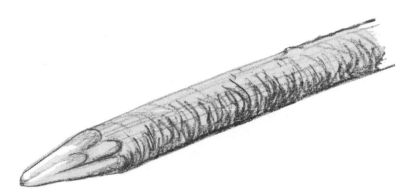

Figure 3

4. Whittle the branches and sand them smooth. Then taper one end of each branch, as shown in Fig. 3.

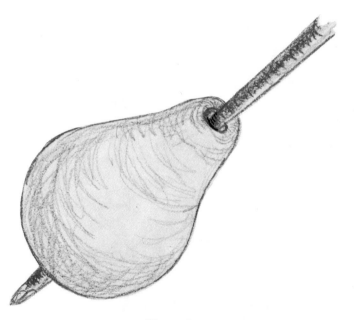

Figure 4

5. Insert each branch through each gourd, as shown in Fig. 4.

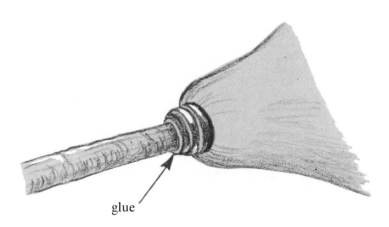

glue

Figure 5

6. Cut the twine in half and wrap each length around each branch, as shown in Fig. 5. Seal the ends of the twine with a coat of white glue.

7. When the glue has dried thoroughly, paint the gourds. When the paint has dried, draw a design on each gourd. You can use one of the designs shown in Fig. 6. or at the end of this chapter. Paint the design with contrasting colors. If you use tempera paint, you will need to spray the gourds with a protective finish.

Figure 6

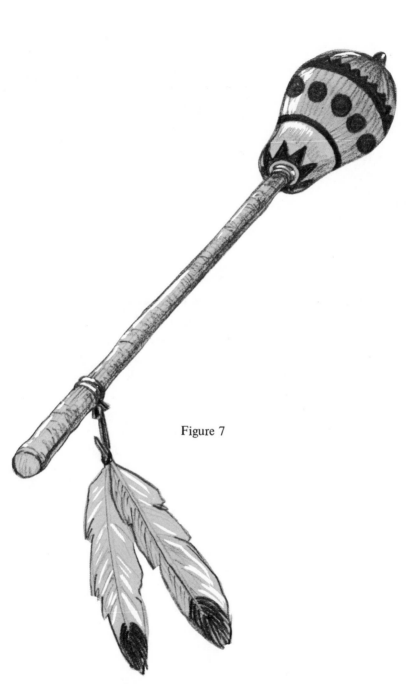

Figure 7

8. Tie the feathers to the handles, as shown in Fig. 7.

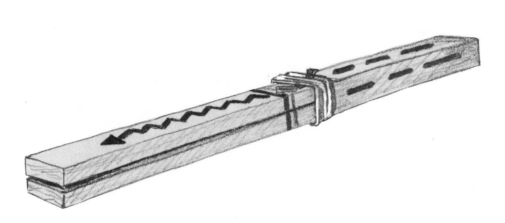

CLAPPER

The music of the California Indians, as well as the tribes of the Pacific Northwest, included drums, musical rasps, rattles, and baskets scraped with sticks. Split-stick clappers were also featured accompaniments to many ceremonial dances and war chants. A clapper is made from a piece of wood, split up the middle for about two-thirds of its length.

A clapper should be gripped in one hand by its handle and slapped against the palm of the other hand. It will make a rather loud clap, and with a minimum of practice, you can produce a variety of interesting rhythms.

Materials
1 piece of baluster molding, 1 1/8" × 1 1/8"
   × 12"
strong cord, 18" long
handsaw
pencil
sharp penknife
ruler
white glue
scissors
acrylic paint and paint brush (optional)

1. Wrap the cord around the baluster molding at a point 3″ from one end, as shown in Fig. 1.

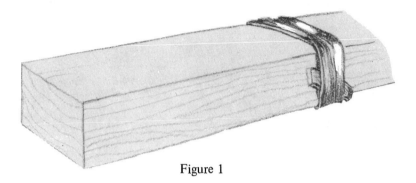

Figure 1

2. Seal the ends of the cord with a coat of glue.

3. When the glue is thoroughly dry, saw the molding, as shown in Fig. 2. The wood inside the split can be shaved carefully so that the two pieces no longer fit together tightly, as shown.

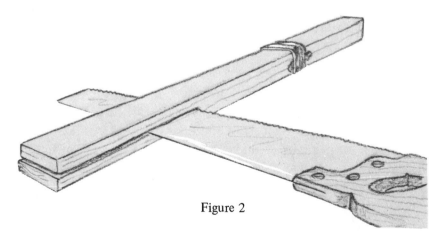

Figure 2

4. The string and the handle of the clapper can be painted or left as is.

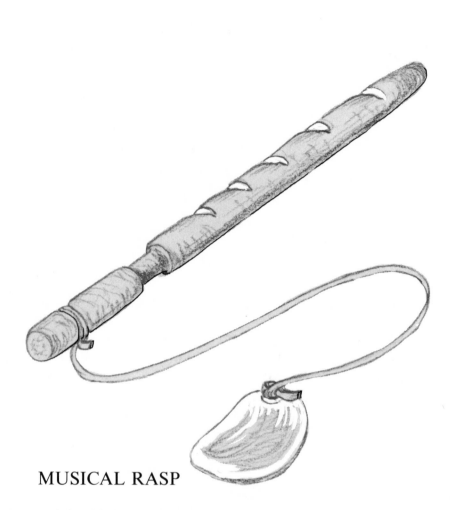

MUSICAL RASP

Other kinds of noisemakers were also used by the Indians. One of the most common was a notched stick along which another stick or a bone (the shoulderblade of a deer, for example) was drawn to make a noise in whatever rhythms were desired. Sometimes the rasp, or ceremonial scraping stick, was supported on a big, hollow gourd or on an upended bowl or pot. This made the noise louder and gave it resonance. Among the Indians of the Southwest, this instrument was called a *morache*—a Spanish word adopted by the tribes from the Mexicans.

You can duplicate this notched-stick instrument. But the noise it makes will vary, depending on how deeply you cut the notches, how close together they are, and how rapidly you rake a piece of bone across the wood.

Materials

1 wooden dowel, 15″ long and 3/4″ in diameter
1 shin bone (ask your butcher for a beef, lamb, or
   veal bone)
leather thong, 24″ long
scissors
sharp penknife
medium sandpaper
drill
3/16″ bit

1. Whittle the dowel, as shown in Fig. 1.

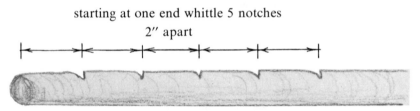

starting at one end whittle 5 notches
2″ apart

Figure 1

2. Whittle a handle for the dowel and taper the other end, as shown in Fig. 2. Sand smooth.

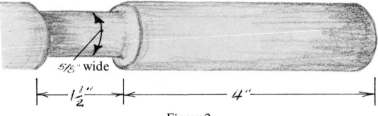

5/8″ wide

1½″   4″

Figure 2

3. Carve a notch in the handle of the dowel, as shown in Fig. 3.

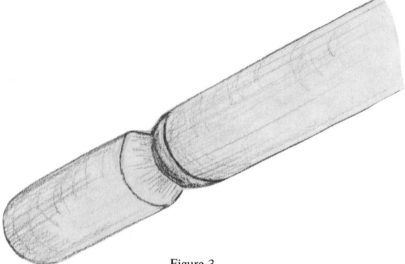

Figure 3

4. Clean the bone, if necessary. When it is thoroughly dry, sand smooth. Drill a hole in one end of the bone, as shown in Fig. 4.

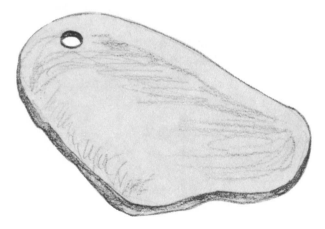

Figure 4

5. Tie one end of the leather thong to the handle of the morache. Pull the other end of the thong through the hole in the bone, as shown in Fig. 5. Fasten securely.

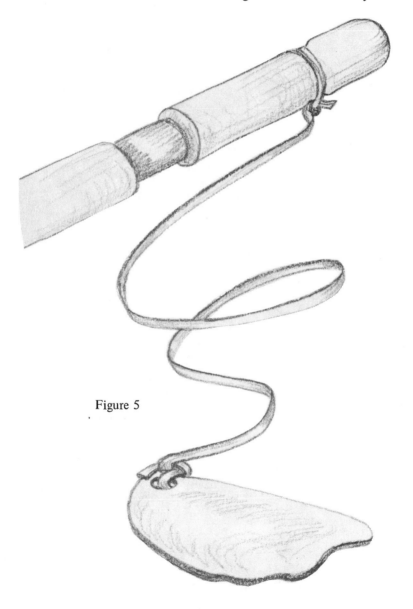

Figure 5

BULL ROARER

Many tribes used bull roarers, also known as rain-making instruments and lightning sticks. They produced a noise which was supposed to duplicate the sound of the thunderbird who caused lightning, thunder, and rain. Many tribes of the plains and prairie regions painted their bull roarers with symbolic designs. The Hopi painted lightning shafts on their

70

bull roarers and used the instruments in their rain-dance ceremonies. When the ceremonies had ended, the bull roarers became the prized toys of Hopi children.

A typical bull roarer consisted of a flat, rectangular piece of wood, notched at one end and suspended from a rawhide thong. When the Indians whirled the bull roarers around their heads, the pieces of wood fluttered in the air and made loud, whirring nosies.

Materials
2″ × 1/2″ piece of common pine, 12″ long
3 yards of cord
1 branch, 4″ long and approximately 1/2″ in
    diameter
sharp penknife
drill
3/16″ bit
scissors
acrylic paints
brush

1. Whittle the pine and drill a hole in one end, as shown in Fig. 1.

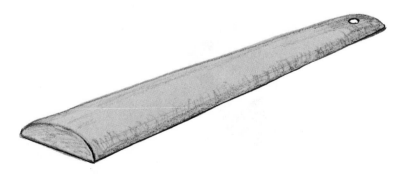

Figure 1

2. Paint a design on the surface of the wood. You may use one of the designs shown in Fig. 2 or at the end of this chapter.

Figure 2

3. Cut the cord into three pieces, each 36″ long. Take the ends of each of the pieces and knot them together. Braid the cords, as shown in Fig. 3. Knot the other ends of the cord, as indicated.

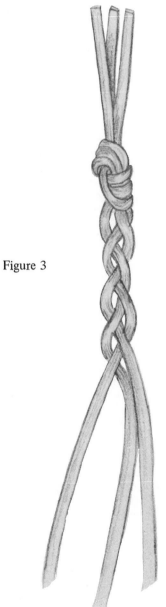

Figure 3

4. Insert one end of the braided cords into the hole in the wooden piece, as shown in Fig. 4. Tie securely.

Figure 4

5. Whittle a notch near the end of the branch, as shown in Fig. 5.

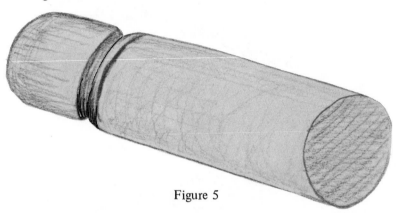

Figure 5

6. Tie the remaining end of the braided cords around the notch and fasten securely, as shown in Fig. 6.

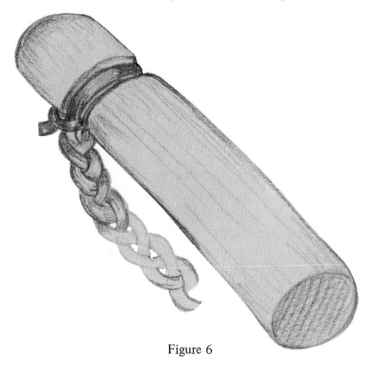

Figure 6

JINGLER ANKLETS

The rhythmical, melodious sound of jingling objects were important parts of the ceremonial dance music of many tribes, especially those in the Northeast and the Lakes regions. Each jingler consisted of two flat, cone-shaped pieces of carved shell, horn, or bone. From thirty to forty pairs of jinglers were fastened to a rawhide thong, which the Indians tied just below their knees or around their ankles. When the Indians danced, the jinglers emitted a tinkling noise that accompanied the beat of drums. In later years, when tin, brass, and copper found their way into Indian

76

settlements, jingler anklets were cut and molded from tin cans and other metal containers. These jinglers closely resembled the jingle bells we use for Christmas ornaments.

Materials
piece of firm rawhide, 1 3/4″ × 8″
leather thong, 36″ long
6 small jingle bells with shanks
sharp penknife
pencil
ruler
scissors

1. Measure and mark eight spaces on the rawhide, as shown in Fig. 1.

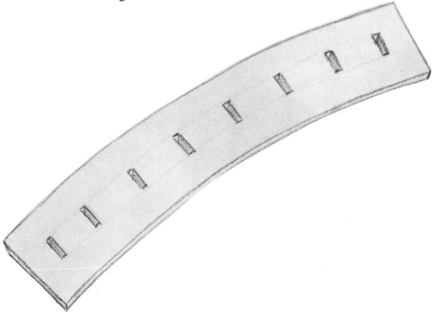

Figure 1

2. Slit the rawhide with a knife at the points indicated in Fig. 2.

you will have to make 2 slits about
3/16″ apart and cut out the small piece of rawhide

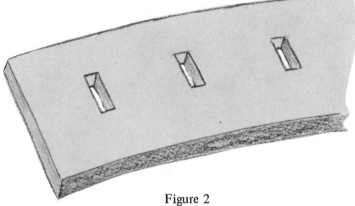

Figure 2

3. Insert the shanks of the bells through the slits in the rawhide, as shown in Fig. 3.

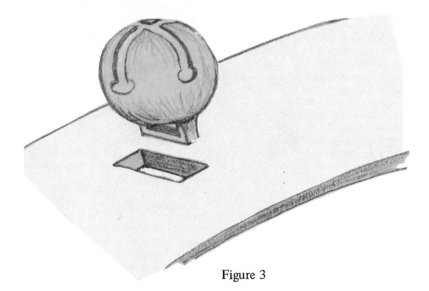

Figure 3

4. Slip the leather thong through the shank of each bell, as shown in Fig. 4.

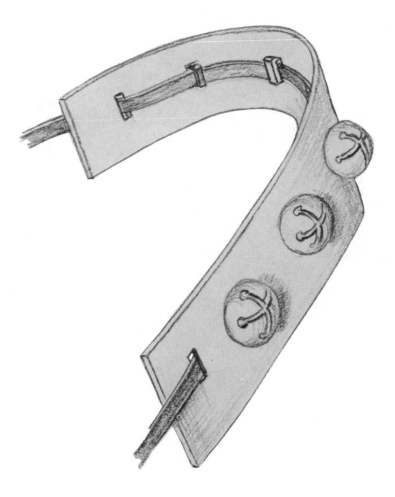

Figure 4

Note: the length of the piece of rawhide can be shortened, according to the circumference measurement of the wearer's leg or ankle.

DOUBLE-HEAD DRUM

An Indian drum consisted of a hollow cylinder or container over which a cover, or head, made of hide or similar material, was tightly stretched. The head was always beaten with one or more drumsticks. (American Indians rarely used their hands when playing drums.) Some Indian drums, called tom-toms, were small enough to be held in the hand. Other drums were giant cylinders made of hollow logs as long as ten feet. These were supported on stakes and thumped simultaneously by several Indians. Many southwestern tribes used clay pots of various sizes and shapes for their drum cylinders, some of which they partially filled with water. Three main types of drums were used by the Indians. The most commonly used was the small, double-head drum. It was easily carried about and was often part of a dancer's equipment.

Materials

cardboard cylinder (empty, 3-gallon commercial
    ice cream container or a similar vessel)
2 circles of thin (less than 1/16" thick) rawhide,
    each 2" larger in diameter than the diameter of
    the cylinder
rawhide thong, 8 yards long
sharp penknife
pencil
ruler
hole puncher
hammer
scissors
3 or more waterproof marking pens in various
    colors
acrylic paint and paint brush (optional)

1. Discard the lid of the container. When the container has been thoroughly cleaned and dried, remove the bottom by cutting the cardboard, as shown in Fig. 1. Paint the cylinder, if you wish, and allow the paint to dry. If the cylinder is less than 1/8" thick, cut a piece of tin sheeting (roof flashing) to fit the inside dimensions of the cylinder and line the cylinder.

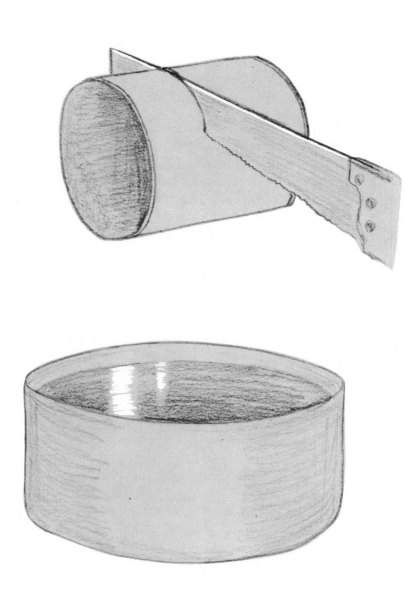

Figure 1

2. Punch two holes in each side of the cylinder (and also the liner, if you are using one), as shown in Fig. 2.

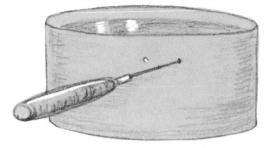

Figure 2

3. Insert the two pieces of thong through the cylinder's holes, as shown in Fig. 3. Knot the thongs on the inside of the cylinder.

Figure 3

4. Mark dots at 2″ intervals around the perimeters of each of the two circles of rawhide, 3/4″ in from the edges, as shown in Fig. 4.

Figure 4

5. Using a hole puncher and a hammer, make holes in the rawhide circles, as shown in Fig. 5. Soak the two rawhide circles in water until thoroughly wet.

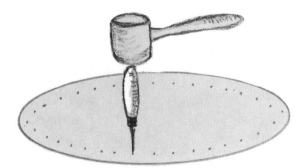

Figure 5

Figure 6

6. Center each of the wet rawhide circles on each end of
   the cylinder, as shown in Fig. 6. Loosely lace the
   rawhide circles together with the remaining length of
   leather thong, as shown in Fig. 7.

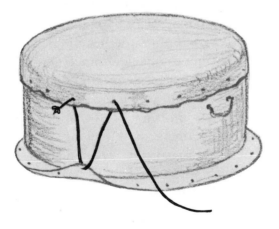

Figure 7

7. Pull the lacing taut, but keep an even tension on the entire perimeter of each rawhide circle, as shown in Fig. 8. Allow the rawhide to dry thoroughly.

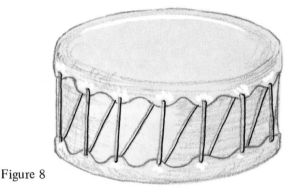

Figure 8

8. Pencil a design on each of the dried rawhide surfaces and color the designs with waterproof marking pens. You can use one of the two designs shown in Fig. 9 or you can choose one of the designs shown at the end of this chapter.

Note: Variations in tone are possible in a double-head drum, but you must decide about this before you lace the rawhide circles in place. Some tribes produced different tones by putting rattlesnake rattles inside the drum cylinders. You can achieve much the same effect by placing a small bag of pebbles or sand inside the drum cylinder. This will soften the sound of the drum. You can decorate your drum by attaching beads, shells, sticks, bells, or feathers to the thong lacing or the carrying strap. Most of the decorations will make additional sounds when the drum is beaten.

(If you wish you may paint your designs on the rawhide before you attach it to the drum.)

Figure 9

DRUMSTICKS

An Indian drumstick was usually made of a slender, tapered stick or branch and decorated with feathers. It was padded at one end, either with rags wrapped around the stick or with small rawhide bags stuffed with moss, fur, or human hair.

Materials

2 wooden dowels, each 1/2″ in diameter and 12″
   long (or 2 straight branches of approximately
   the same size)
strong cord
cotton batting
piece of chamois, 4″ × 8″
4 small feathers
white glue
scissors
ruler
pencil
sharp penknife
medium sandpaper

1. Whittle each dowel, or branch, as shown in Fig. 1, and
   sand it smooth.

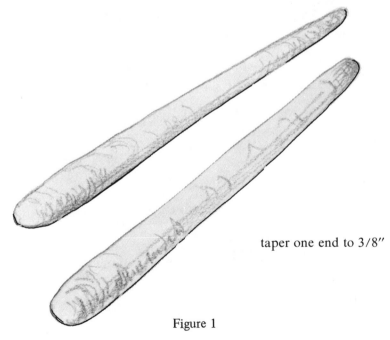

taper one end to 3/8″

Figure 1

2. Cut two circles, each 4″ in diameter, from the 4″ × 8″ piece of chamois. Wrap each piece around the end of each dowel, as shown in Fig. 2.

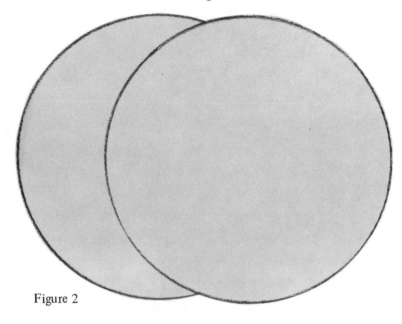

Figure 2

3. Place the cotton stuffing inside each of the chamois circles and secure with cord, as shown in Fig. 3.

Figure 3

4. Using cord and glue, attach two feathers to the handles of each of the drumsticks, as shown in Fig. 4

Figure 4

BAMBOO FLUTE

Nearly every North American tribe had two wind instruments: the flute and the whistle. Whistles, used only for signalling purposes, were usually made of the long wing-bones of large birds, such as eagles and hawks. Flutes were made of cedar and other woods, including bamboo. Two soft overnotes could be coaxed from a bamboo flute, making it possible to play a tune within a one-octave range. Indian flutes, often called flageolets, were most commonly played by young braves when they courted and serenaded Indian maidens. Although the instruments were seldom used in tribal ceremonies, warriors often substituted flutes for whistles in order to signal directions to each other during battles.

Materials

piece of bamboo, 1 1/4″ in diameter and 18″
  long
hardwood, 1″ × 2″ × 5/8″
cardboard or stiff vinyl, 2″ × 5/8″
  (approximately 1/32″ thick)
rawhide thong, 24″ long
2 small feathers
sharp penknife
3/4″ dowel, 1/2″ long
ruler
pencil
flat rasp
drill
1/2″, 1/4″, and 1/8″ bits
scissors
white glue

1. Using a 1/2″ bit, drill out one of the inner walls of the bamboo and trim the ridges in the wood, as shown in Fig. 1.

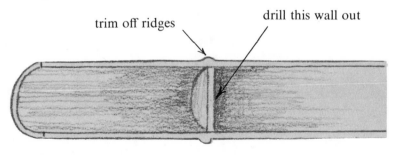

trim off ridges

drill this wall out

Figure 1   cut away view

2. File a flat section with the rasp, as shown in Fig. 2.

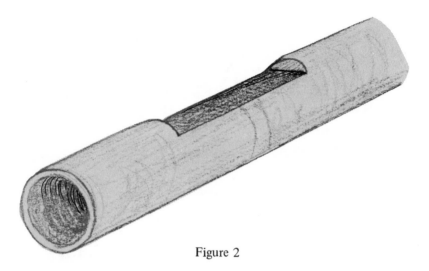

Figure 2

3. With a sharp penknife, carefully cut two holes on either side of the vertical rib, as shown in Fig. 3. Be sure to cut the angle on one side of the rib, as indicated.

cut away view

Figure 3

4. Drill 1/4″ holes in the bamboo, according to Fig. 4.

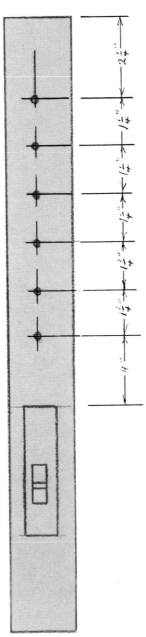

Figure 4

5. Cut the piece of cardboard or vinyl for the flute's volume control, as shown in Fig. 5.

Figure 5

6. Cut the piece of hardwood, according to Fig. 6. Make sure the bottom of the wood is perfectly flat. Sand the piece smooth.

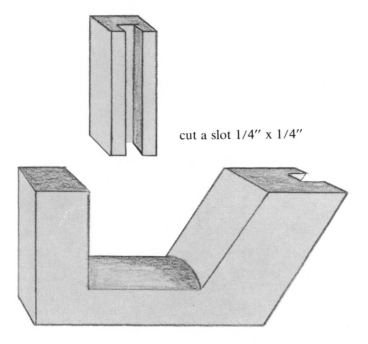

cut a slot 1/4″ x 1/4″

Figure 6

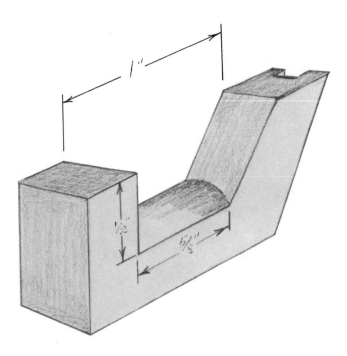

7. Drill a 1/8″ hole in the 3/4″ dowel. Whittle it, if
   necessary, so that it will fit inside the end of the
   bamboo, as shown in Fig. 7. Glue the dowel in place.

trim here if necessary

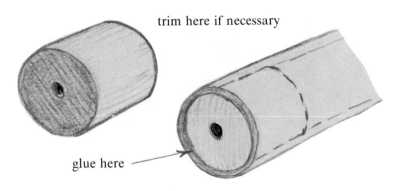

glue here

Figure 7

8. Shift the volume control piece and the hardwood piece back and forth, while blowing into them to check the tone, as shown in Fig. 8. When you have the best possible tone, tie the two pieces in place.

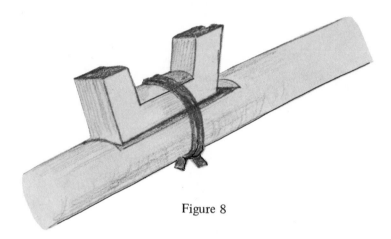

Figure 8

9. Wind the thong around the bamboo and tie, as shown in Fig. 9.

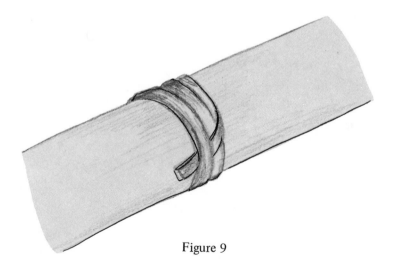

Figure 9

10.　Attach the feathers, as shown in Fig. 10.

Figure 10

DESIGNS FOR DECORATING
INDIAN MUSICAL INSTRUMENTS

Pueblo

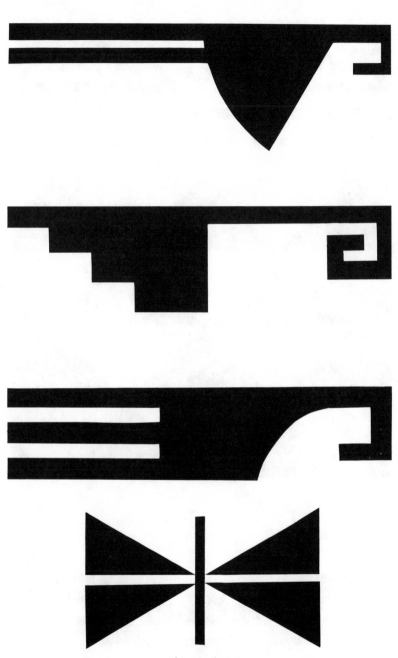

Arapaho

Yurok

Navajo

Osage

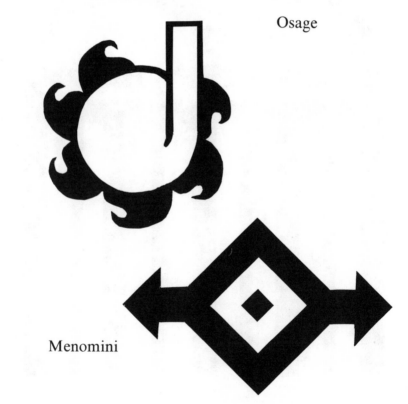

Menomini

Apache

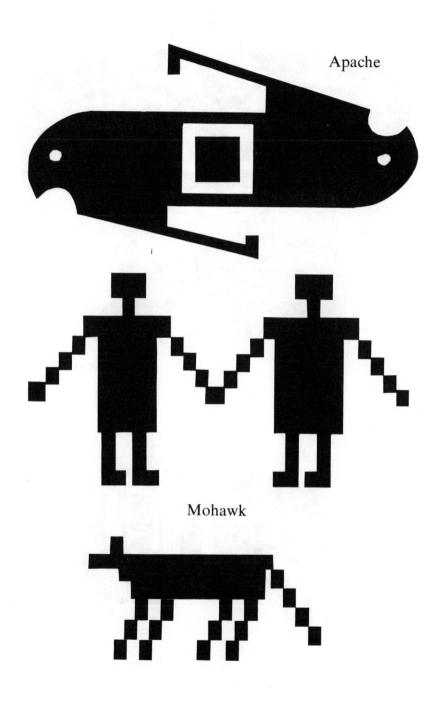

Mohawk

Tlinglit

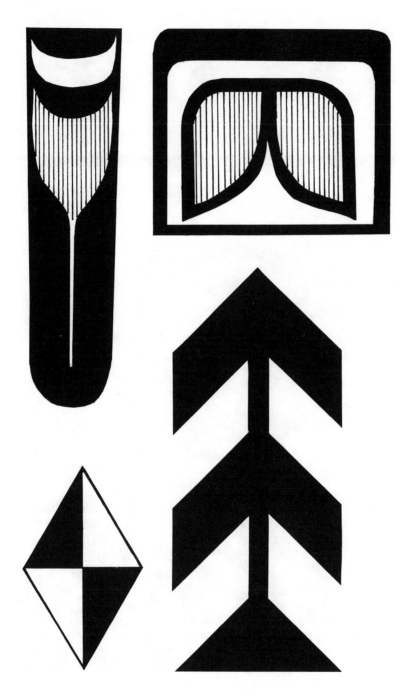

107

Zuni

Hopi

Pima

Iroquois

COMMON METRIC EQUIVALENTS AND CONVERSIONS

Approximate

1 inch	= 25 millimeters
1 foot	= 0.3 meter
1 yard	= 0.9 meter
1 square inch	= 6.5 square centimeters
1 square foot	= 0.09 square meter
1 square yard	= 0.8 square meter
1 millimeter	= 0.04 inch
1 meter	= 3.3 feet
1 meter	= 1.1 yards
1 square centimeter	= 0.16 square inch

Accurate to Parts Per Million

inches $\times$ 25.4	= millimeters
feet $\times$ 0.3048	= meters
yards $\times$ 0.9144	= meters
square inches $\times$ 6.4516	= square centimeters
square feet $\times$ 0.092903	= square meters
square yards $\times$ 0.836127	= square meters

Selected Bibliography

Austin, Mary. *The American Rhythm.* New York: Harcourt, Brace and Co., 1923

Buttree, Julia M. (Julia M. Seton). *The Rhythm of the Redman.* New York: A. S. Barnes, 1930.

Curtis, Natalie. *The Indians' Book.* New York: Harper and Brothers, 1923. Republished by Dover Publications, Inc., 1968.

Densmore, Frances. *Study of Indian Music.* Washington: Smithsonian Institution, 1941.

Hodge, Frederick W. *Handbook of American Indians North of Mexico.* New York: Rowman and Littlefield, Inc., 1965.

Hunt, W. Ben. *Indian Crafts and Lore.* New York: Golden Press, 1954.

LaFarge, Oliver. *A Pictorial History of the American Indian.* New York: Crown Publishers, Inc., 1956.

LaFarge, Oliver. *The American Indian.* New York: Golden Press, 1960.

Parker, Arthur C. *The Indian How Book.* New York: George H. Doran Co., 1927.

Schneider, Richard C. *Crafts of the North American Indians.* New York: Van Nostrand Reinhold Co., 1972.

Tunis, Edwin. *Indians.* Cleveland: The World Publishing Co., 1959.

Whiteford, Andrew Hunter. *North American Indian Arts.* New York: Golden Press, 1974.

Index

Alaska, 2
Apache, 18, 53
Arapaho, 45

Bering Strait, 2
Box drum, 14
Bull roarer, 70

California Indians, ix, 64
Canadian Sub-Arctic, xi
Central America, xi, 2
Cheyenne, 23, 28, 29, 44
Chippewa, 37
Clapper, 16, 64
Columbus, 1

Corn-dance song, 40
Corn-grinding songs, 40
Crop songs, 37
Curtis, Natalie, 6

Dakota Sioux, 17, 22, 31, 35,
   37, 48
Death songs, 51
Densmore, Frances, 6
Designs for decorating Indian
   musical instruments, 100
Drums, 12, 13, 14, 27, 34, 84
   decorations, 86
   drumsticks, 88
   variations in tone, 88

113

Europeans, 6, 9

Fiddle, 18
Flageolet, 92
Flute, 17, 92

Gourd rattle, 15, 58
Great Spirit, 4, 11, 27, 29, 30

Happy hunting ground, 51
Hopi, 39, 43, 70, 100
Hunting songs, 37

Indians (general):
  arrival in America, 2
  beliefs, 4
  customs, 4
  languages, 3
  musical instruments, 12
    how to make, 55
  physical features, 5
  population of, 2
  tribes, major in N. A., ix
    number of, 3
  voice for singing, 11
  women, 11, 20, 30, 31, 43, 44,
    48
Iroquois, 103

Jingler ankets, 76
Joyful songs, 19

Kiowa, 29, 30, 45, 48

Lakes, x, 76
Love songs, 47
Lullabies, 43

Maidu, 18
Malecite, 19, 47

Medicine, 33
  man, 34
Menomini, 102
Metric equivalents and
  conversions, 110
Mexico, 3
Mohawk, 104
Morache, 66

Navajo, 25, 35, 38, 101
Notched stick, 15, 66
Northeast, xi, 76

Pacific Northwest, ix, 12, 14, 16,
  64
Panpipes, 17
Pawnee, 28, 30
Peru, 2
Plains, x
Plateau-Basin, ix
Prairie, x
Pueblo, 39, 100

Rasp, 66
Rattles, 15, 34, 58
"Redskins," 4

Seton, Ernest Thompson, 52
Shaman, 34, 41
Siberia, 2
Sioux, 31, 37
Songs, 1, 6, 9
  ceremonial, 10, 11
  contests, 12
  crop, 37
  death, 51
  hunting, 3
  joy, 19
  love, 47
  lullabies, 43

medicine, 33
ownership, 10
purpose, 9
sorrow, 19
sources, 10
war, 27
Sorrow songs, 19
South America, 2
Southeast, x
South Pacific, 2
Southwest, ix, 14, 16, 17, 39, 66

Tombe, 13

Tom-tom, 13, 34, 80

War drums, 27
War songs, 27
Water drum, 14, 52
Weddings, 19
Whistle, 17, 92
Winnebago, 28, 49

Yuma, 24
Yurok, 105

Zuñi, 20, 21,39

781.7
Fic
                              16222

AUTHOR		
Fichter, George S.		
TITLE Amer. Indian music and musical instruments		
DATE DUE	BORROWER'S NAME	ROOM NUMBER
OCT 18	Martin Kernan	i2